Excellent English

CW00419963

Contents   Page

A Guide to Excellent Writing

Many students struggle to write clearly and effectively which has a negative effect on their marks. Writing clearly is one of the most important skills that you'll need to excel in your examinations for not just the 11+ but for SATs, GCSEs and more!

Here are some things that you can do to improve your writing and instantly boost your marks.

Write Clearly

As you write, think about how the words and sentences sound in your head. Your writing should be easy for you and others to read so try reading your work to yourself or someone you know. As you do this you'll instantly be able to spot mistakes and make corrections.

One mistake that many students make is that they assume that just because they understand their work, others will too. Remember that although you might understand what you're trying to say, the person reading your work might not. This is why it's very important to make sure that your sentences are well structured and understandable. You only have one chance to impress the reader (who might be a teacher or examiner) which means that you should put lots of effort into writing a story that is interesting and easy to read.

Be Descriptive

Sentences that have no description can be very boring for the reader. In the 11+, SATs and 13+ writing exams, teachers will award marks to students whose work is detailed and descriptive.

One way to add more description is to make the best use of your vocabulary. For example, if you're about to use a word like 'good' to describe someone, replace it with a word that is far more detailed and tells us more about the character you're writing about. Is the person just *good* or are they *polite, kind, enthusiastic, compassionate, smart* or *exemplary*?

Describing someone as good doesn't really tell us much about their personality, their morals or what they value? However, the word *compassionate* tells us more. See how easy it is to use more specific vocabulary?

Use Your Imagination

Writing an interesting and unique composition requires being creative. Before you begin writing why not think of some unique or original ideas that will help to make your work stand out? A great way of expanding your imagination is to write down some ideas. You could even create a little book of imaginative ideas and add new ideas to the book so that you don't forget them.

Ask Questions

Rhetorical questions are an excellent way of making your writing more compelling. By simply asking your reader questions, you can get the reader to think more deeply about a topic. For instance, a question like 'do you know how much water the average person drinks every day?' would be excellent in a writing composition about healthy eating or wasting water. Can you think of any questions you can add to your

 © Excellent English 2012. www.ignitetuition.co.uk

writing? If so, go ahead and include them because they will make a big difference to your work.

Show Off Your Grammar!

A lot of people underestimate how many grammatical terms they know and forget to show their grammatical knowledge when writing. Remember that verbs, adjectives, adverbs and connectives are all brilliant grammatical terms that can be used to make your writing more detailed and will help to boost your marks.

Don't forget to show off your writing skills and write in a way that is clear, detailed and interesting. Write work that you'd want to read!

The following writing tasks (called compositions) have been designed to help you improve your writing and get used to writing high standard compositions.

The titles are meant to help stimulate ideas for the types of stories you can write about. You can of course write about almost anything you like so far as it is relevant to the title.

 © Excellent English 2012. www.ignitetuition.co.uk

Writing Compositions

Here are some ideas for writing compositions. Use the titles below to come up with your own interesting and exciting compositions. The more compositions you write, the better you'll be!

- The Escape
- My Favourite Memory
- The Fear
- The Lost Land
- Magic Words
- The Dream
- A Nightmare World
- The Secret Code
- Snakes!
- The Hidden Garden
- The Prisoner
- Dear Diary
- Diary of a Naughty Kid
- The Happiest Day Ever!
- The Magician's Code
- The Witch Hunt
- Finding Fun
- My New Friend
- The Hairdresser
- My Evil Friend
- The Zoo
- Babysitting My Brother

 © Excellent English 2012. www.ignitetuition.co.uk

Letter Writing Ideas

1. Write a letter to a pen-pal who lives in a different country. Tell them about life in your country and ask them interesting questions about themselves.

2. Imagine you are the school prefect. Write a letter to your head teacher telling them about things that could be improved in your school.

3. Write a letter to your local politician asking him or her to make three changes to your local area. For example, would you like to see schools improve, cleaner streets or more parks? Remember to use rhetorical questions and adjectives to make your writing very engaging.

4. Write a letter to a friend persuading them to visit your school. Why should they visit? Is something interesting happening? What's a typical day like in your school?

5. The head teacher has asked you to apply to become head boy or head girl. Write a letter to your class teacher asking him or her to let you give a speech to your classmates. You could even include a sample or example of the speech you'll make.

Try writing at least 2 pages for each composition piece.

How To Answer Comprehension Questions

Comprehensions test your ability to read and understand information.

One big mistake that many students make when answering comprehensions is that they don't focus on the information that's in front of them. Remember that all of the information on an exam or practice paper is designed to help you! Focus on what's right in front of you by making sure that you read through the text and questions properly.

Another big mistake that many students make is that they get distracted and start thinking about things that aren't even on the comprehension! Don't lose focus and pay attention to what the story, article or poem says.

When completing comprehensions sometimes it's good to be tactical. In other words, create a strategy or method that works for you and that allows you to answer the questions in a way that helps you to maximise the number of marks you get. For example, one strategy that I teach to my students is the
1-2-3 method.

The **1-2-3 method** works like this:

      (Step 1) Read through the questions first.

      (Step 2) Read the comprehension text.

      (Step 3) Read through the comprehension again but this time highlight the answers to the questions.

 © Excellent English 2012. www.ignitetuition.co.uk

For each highlighted quote or section, write the question number next to the text so that when you finally put the answers down it will be very quick and easy.

If the answer is not in the text (for example a synonym question) simply move on and highlight the next answer. Once all of your highlighting is complete, answer the questions. Don't forget to answer the questions that don't have highlighted answers!

When it comes to comprehensions and compositions, the better your vocabulary, the easier you'll find answering any type of English exam question to a high standard. Vocabulary simply means knowing the meaning (or definitions) behind the words you see. For example, do you know what the word 'avaricious' means?

The best ways to increase your vocabulary and learn new words is to:

Read more

Don't just stick to reading one type of book. Read a variety of types within different genres. For example, you could read a book about magic and then read a book about a key historical figure. By mixing up the types of books you read, the more you'll come across a wider range of vocabulary which means you'll improve your knowledge and do better in exams!

Read classic books

The comprehension in this book consists of extracts from some of the world's greatest writers. We've chosen to use classic books for a reason. They contain stories that are some of the most treasured in the world and are filled with weird and wonderful words that you should learn if you want to have excellent vocabulary.

646 477 0664

Use a dictionary

Dictionaries and thesauruses are brilliant because they're filled with hundreds of incredible words. Whenever you see a word that you don't know, simply check it's meaning in a dictionary and then learn the definition. Thesauruses are great for helping you to find alternatives to words you already know and this makes them perfect for story-writing. For example, if you've been repeating the word 'good' you could use a thesaurus to find alternative words.

 © Excellent English 2012. www.ignitetuition.co.uk

Alice's Adventures in Wonderland by Lewis Caroll

Alice was beginning to get very tired of sitting by her sister on the bank, and of having nothing to do. Once or twice she had peeped into the book her sister was reading, but it had no pictures or conversations in it," what is the use of a book," thought Alice, "without pictures or conversation?"

So she was considering in her own mind (as well as she could, for the hot day made her feel very sleepy and stupid), whether the pleasure of making a daisy-chain would be worth the trouble of getting up and picking the daisies, when suddenly a White Rabbit with pink eyes ran close by her.

There was nothing so very remarkable in that; nor did Alice think it so very much out of the way to hear the Rabbit say to itself, "Oh dear! Oh dear! I shall be late!" (when she thought it over afterwards, it occurred to her that she ought to have wondered at this, but at the time it all seemed quite natural); but when the Rabbit actually took a watch out of its waistcoat pocket and looked at it, and then hurried on, Alice started to her feet, for it flashed across her mind that she had never before seen a rabbit with either a waistcoat-pocket, or a watch to take out of it, and burning with curiosity, she ran across the field after it, and fortunately was just in time to see it pop down a large rabbit-hole under the hedge.

In another moment down went Alice after it, never once considering how in the world she was to get out again.

The rabbit-hole went straight on like a tunnel for some way, and then dipped suddenly down, so suddenly that Alice had not a moment to think about stopping herself before she found herself falling down a very deep well.

 © Excellent English 2012. www.ignitetuition.co.uk

Answer the following questions

1. Alice was tired of (circle **one**): (1 mark)

   a. Being near her sister and sitting by the bank

   b. Having nothing to do and sitting by her sister

   c. Reading books with no pictures

   d. Talking to herself

2. The story's protagonist was intrigued by the white rabbit. (2 marks)

   a. What does the word 'protagonist' mean?

   _____

   b. Who is the protagonist in this story?

   _____

3. Alice saw the rabbit looking at its watch. Using your own words, describe how she felt. (3 marks)

   _____

   _____

4. What does the phrase, '**burning with curiosity**' mean? (3 marks)

   _____

   _____

   _____

   _____

 © Excellent English 2012. www.ignitetuition.co.uk

5. Alice thought that the book was useless because it lacked: (1 mark)

  a. Adjectives and images

  b. Comprehension and images

  c. Dialogue and images

  d. Conversation and comprehension

Writing Task

Complete each of the compositions below. Each composition should take you **30 minutes**.

- Once Alice falls down the well, what happens? Write a short story that describes what happens to her next.   *(10 marks)*

- Who is Alice? Write a detailed description of what you think Alice looks and behaves like.   *(10 marks)*

- The white rabbit certainly seems to be an interesting character. Write a 1-2 page account about what makes the white rabbit unique.   *(10 marks)*

I scored: _____

Adventures in Kensington Gardens by Sir James Barrie

Sometimes the little boy who calls me father brings me an invitation from his mother: "I shall be so pleased if you will come and see me," and I always reply in some such words as these: "Dear madam, I decline." And if David asks why I decline, I explain that it is because I have no desire to meet the woman.

"Come this time, father," he urged lately, "for it is her birthday, and she is twenty-six," which is so great an age to David that I think he fears she cannot last much longer.

"Twenty-six, is she, David?" I replied. "Tell her I said she looks more."

I had a delicious dream that night. I dreamt that I too was twenty-six, which was a long time ago, and that I took train to a place called my home, whose whereabouts I see not in my waking hours, and when I alighted at the station a dear lost love was waiting for me, and we went away together. She met me in no ecstasy of emotion, nor was I surprised to find her there; it was as if we had been married for years and parted for a day. I like to think that I gave her some of the things to carry.

Were I to tell my delightful dream to David's mother, to whom I have never in my life addressed one word, she would droop her head and raise it bravely, to imply that I make her very sad but very proud, and she would be wishful to lend me her absurd little pocket handkerchief. And then, had I the heart, I might make a disclosure that would startle her, for it is not the face of David's mother that I see in my dreams.

Has it ever been your lot, reader, to be persecuted by a pretty woman who thinks, without a tittle of reason that you are bowed down under a

 © Excellent English 2012. www.ignitetuition.co.uk

hopeless partiality for her? It is thus that I have been pursued for several years now by the unwelcome sympathy of the tender-hearted and virtuous Mary A---- When we pass in the street the poor deluded soul subdues her buoyancy, as if it were shame to walk happy before one she has lamed, and at such times the rustle of her gown is whispered words of comfort to me, and her arms are kindly wings that wish I was a little boy like David. I also detect in her a fearful elation, which I am unaware of until she has passed, when it comes back to me like a faint note of challenge. Eyes that say you never must, a nose that says, 'why don't you?' A mouth that says, 'I rather wish you could.' Such is the portrait of Mary A---- as she and I pass by.

Once she dared to address me, so that she could boast to David that I had spoken to her. I was in the Kensington Gardens, and she asked would I tell her the time please, just as children ask, and forget as they run back with it to their nurse. But I was prepared even for this, and raising my hat I pointed with my staff to a clock in the distance. She should have been overwhelmed, but as I walked on listening intently, I thought with displeasure that I heard her laughing.

Her laugh is very like David's, whom I could punch all day in order to hear him laugh. I dare say she put this laugh into him. She has been putting qualities into David, altering him, turning him forever on a lathe since the day she first knew him, and indeed long before, and all so deftly that he is still called a child of nature.

 © Excellent English 2012. www.ignitetuition.co.uk

Answer the following questions

1. Who is David to the narrator?   **(1 mark)**

_____

2. Why does David want his father to visit his mother?   **(1 mark)**

   a. Because he fears she is becoming old
   b. Because he fears she might run away
   c. Because he fears she might die soon
   d. Because he thinks she's becoming old

3. The fathers' response to David's mother is: **(1 mark)**

   a. Polite
   b. Cantankerous
   c. Pleasant
   d. Diplomatic

4. In your own words describe what the phrase, '***subdues her buoyancy***' means.   **(3 marks)**

_____

_____

_____

5. Why would the narrator want to punch David all day?   **(3 marks)**

_____

_____

 © Excellent English 2012. www.ignitetuition.co.uk

6. Suggest **one** reason why the narrator dislikes David's mother.

(1 marks)

_____

_____

_____

Writing Task

Complete each of the compositions below:

Write a story called, 'Two Friends.'   **(10 marks)**

It can be about anything to do with friendship.

Use your imagination to make it as interesting as possible.

Describe a dream.   **(10 marks)**

Imagine you are David. Write a letter to both of your parents pleading them to be friends.   **(10 marks)**

I scored: _____

Cyclone Cellar by L. Frank Baum

Dorothy lived in the midst of the great Kansas prairies, with Uncle Henry, who was a farmer, and Aunt Em, who was the farmer's wife. Their house was small, for the lumber to build it had to be carried by wagon many miles. There were four walls, a floor and a roof, which made one room; and this room contained a rusty looking cook-stove, a cupboard for the dishes, a table, three or four chairs, and the beds. Uncle Henry and Aunt Em had a big bed in one corner, and Dorothy a little bed in another corner. There was no garret at all, and no cellar--except a small hole dug in the ground, called a cyclone cellar, where the family could go in case one of those great whirlwinds arose, mighty enough to crush any building in its path. It was reached by a trap door in the middle of the floor, from which a ladder led down into the small, dark hole.

When Dorothy stood in the doorway and looked around, she could see nothing but the great grey prairie on every side. Nor a tree nor a house broke the broad sweep of flat country that reached to the edge of the sky in all directions. The sun had baked the ploughed land into a grey mass, with little cracks running through it. Even the grass was not green, for the sun had burned the tops of the long blades until they were the same grey colour to be seen everywhere. Once the house had been painted, but the sun blistered the paint and the rains washed it away, and now the house was as dull and grey as everything else. When Aunt Em came there to live she was a young, pretty wife. The sun and wind had changed her, too. They had taken the sparkle from her eyes and left them a sober grey; they had taken the red from her cheeks and lips, and they were grey also. She was thin and gaunt, and never smiled now. When Dorothy, who was an orphan, first came to her, Aunt Em had been so startled by the child's

 © Excellent English 2012. www.ignitetuition.co.uk

laughter that she would scream and press her hand upon her heart whenever Dorothy's merry voice reached her ears; and she still looked at the little girl with wonder that she could find anything to laugh at.

Uncle Henry never laughed. He worked hard from morning till night and did not know what joy was. He was grey also, from his long beard to his rough boots, and he looked stern and solemn, and rarely spoke. It was Toto that made Dorothy laugh, and saved her from growing as grey as her other surroundings. Toto was not grey; he was a little black dog, with long silky hair and small black eyes that twinkled merrily on either side of his funny, wee nose. Toto played all day long, and Dorothy played with him, and loved him dearly.

Today, however, they were not playing. Uncle Henry sat upon the doorstep and looked anxiously at the sky, which was even greyer than usual. Dorothy stood in the door with Toto in her arms, and looked at the sky too. Aunt Em was washing the dishes.

From the far north they heard a low wail of the wind, and Uncle Henry and Dorothy could see where the long grass bowed in waves before the coming storm. There now came a sharp whistling in the air from the south, and as they turned their eyes that way they saw ripples in the grass coming from that direction also.

Suddenly Uncle Henry stood up.

 © Excellent English 2012. www.ignitetuition.co.uk

Answer the following questions

1) What is a prairie? **(1 mark)**

_____

_____

2) Where does Dorothy live? **(1 mark)**

_____

_____

3) Explain in your own words the meaning of the following phrase:

"The sun had baked the ploughed land into a grey mass, with little cracks running through it." **(2 marks)**

_____

_____

_____

4) Write down three examples of alliterative phrases that are used in this extract. **(2 marks)**

_____

_____

_____

 © Excellent English 2012. www.ignitetuition.co.uk

5) The sun is presented as being a very powerful force within the lives of the characters. What effect has the sun had on Aunt Em, Uncle Henry and their farm?

(4 marks)

_____

_____

_____

_____

_____

Writing Task

Imagine that Dorothy has a cat pet. Describe what the cat looks like and how it behaves.   **(10 marks)**

Imagine that the Uncle Henry, Aunt Em, Dorothy and Toto have gone into the cellar to keep safe. Describe what happens to them next.

(10marks)

Write a story about a visit to a family member's house.   **(10 marks)**

I scored: _____

Around The World In 80 Days by Jules Verne

Mr. Phileas Fogg lived, in 1872, at No. 7, Saville Row, Burlington Gardens, the house in which Sheridan died in 1814. He was one of the most noticeable members of the Reform Club, though he seemed always to avoid attracting attention; an enigmatical personage, about whom little was known, except that he was a polished man of the world. People said that he resembled Byron--at least that his head was Byronic; but he was a bearded, tranquil Byron, who might live on a thousand years without growing old.

Certainly an Englishman, it was more doubtful whether Phileas Fogg was a Londoner. He was never seen on 'Change, nor at the Bank, nor in the counting-rooms of the "City;" no ships ever came into London docks of which he was the owner; he had no public employment; he had never been entered at any of the Inns of Court, either at the Temple, or Lincoln's Inn, or Grey's Inn; nor had his voice ever resounded in the Court of Chancery, or in the Exchequer, or the Queen's Bench, or the Ecclesiastical Courts. He certainly was not a manufacturer; nor was he a merchant or a gentleman farmer. His name was strange to the scientific and learned societies, and he never was known to take part in the sage deliberations of the Royal Institution or the London Institution, the Artisan's Association, or the Institution of Arts and Sciences. He belonged, in fact, to none of the numerous societies which swarm in the English capital, from the Harmonic to that of the Entomologists, founded mainly for the purpose of abolishing pernicious insects.

Phileas Fogg was a member of the Reform, and that was all.

The way in which he got admission to this exclusive club was simple enough.

 © Excellent English 2012. www.ignitetuition.co.uk

He was recommended by the Barings, with whom he had an open credit. His cheques were regularly paid at sight from his account current, which was always flush.

Was Phileas Fogg rich? Undoubtedly. But those who knew him best could not imagine how he had made his fortune, and Mr. Fogg was the last person to whom to apply for the information. He was not lavish, nor, on the contrary, avaricious; for, whenever he knew that money was needed for a noble, useful, or benevolent purpose, he supplied it quietly and sometimes anonymously. He was, in short, the least communicative of men. He talked very little, and seemed all the more mysterious for his taciturn manner. His daily habits were quite open to observation; but whatever he did was so exactly the same thing that he had always done before, that the wits of the curious were fairly puzzled.

Had he travelled? It was likely, for no one seemed to know the world more familiarly; there was no spot so secluded that he did not appear to have an intimate acquaintance with it. He often corrected, with a few clear words, the thousand conjectures advanced by members of the club as to lost and unheard-of travellers, pointing out the true probabilities, and seeming as if gifted with a sort of second sight, so often did events justify his predictions. He must have travelled everywhere, at least in the spirit.

It was at least certain that Phileas Fogg had not absented himself from London for many years. Those who were honoured by a better acquaintance with him than the rest, declared that nobody could pretend to have ever seen him anywhere else. His sole pastimes were reading the papers and playing whist. He often won at this game, which, as a silent one, harmonised with his nature; but his winnings never went into his purse, being reserved as a fund for his charities. Mr. Fogg played, not to

 © Excellent English 2012. www.ignitetuition.co.uk

win, but for the sake of playing. The game was in his eyes a contest, a struggle with a difficulty, yet a motionless, unwearying struggle, congenial to his tastes.

Answer the following questions

1)   In which century did Phileas Fogg live?   **(1 mark)**

_____

2)   What was Phileas Fogg's occupation?   **(1 marks)**

_____

_____

3) What does the word 'enigmatical' mean and why is it used to describe Phileas?   **(3 marks)**

_____

_____

_____

_____

4) Why is Phileas compared to Byron? Is Phileas different to Byron in any way?   **(5 marks)**

_____

    © Excellent English 2012. www.ignitetuition.co.uk

_____

_____

_____

5)   List 3 Synonyms for the word 'avaricious.'   **(1 mark)**

_____

6)   List 3 Antonyms for the word 'pernicious.'   **(2 marks)**

_____

7)   Circle the correct meaning for the word 'taciturn.'   **(1 mark)**

- Confident
- Reserved
- Loud
- Impolite

8)   Was Phileas rich? Give a brief explanation for your answer.

(3 marks)

_____

_____

_____

9) Give three reasons that explain why Phileas enjoyed playing whist.

(3 marks)

 © Excellent English 2012. www.ignitetuition.co.uk

_____

_____

_____

I scored: _____

Writing Task

Imagine you are Phileas Fogg. Write a series of diary entries that reveal the truth about Phileas's life. Was he born to a wealthy family or a poor one? Did he really care about charitable causes? Was there a dark side to his persona? Remember to write in first person.   **(10 marks)**

Write about a strange or unusual person who lives a life of mystery. Who are they? Where do they live? What makes them strange? What do they look like? Make sure that your composition is descriptive and engaging.

(10 marks)

Write a story that begins with, **'Covered in a bed of crimson coloured roses, I awoke feeling bedazzled and confused. Gently, I lifted my heavy eyelids to see a sight that would change my life forever....'** Make sure that your story contains action, adventure and mystery.   **(10 marks)**

Through The Looking Glass by Lewis Caroll

One thing was certain, that the white kitten had had nothing to do with it:--it was the black kitten's fault entirely. For the white kitten had been having its face washed by the old cat for the last quarter of an hour (and bearing it pretty well, considering); so you see that it couldn't have had any hand in the mischief.

The way Dinah washed her children's faces was this: first she held the poor thing down by its ear with one paw, and then with the other paw she rubbed its face all over, the wrong way, beginning at the nose: and just now, as I said, she was hard at work on the white kitten, which was lying quite still and trying to purr--no doubt feeling that it was all meant for its good.

But the black kitten had been finished with earlier in the afternoon, and so, while Alice was sitting curled up in a corner of the great arm-chair, half talking to herself and half asleep, the kitten had been having a grand game of romps with the ball of worsted Alice had been trying to wind up, and had been rolling it up and down till it had all come undone again; and there it was, spread over the hearth-rug, all knots and tangles, with the kitten running after its own tail in the middle.

'Oh, you wicked little thing!' cried Alice, catching up the kitten, and giving it a little kiss to make it understand that it was in disgrace. "Really, Dinah ought to have taught you better manners! You ought, Dinah, you know you ought!" she added, looking reproachfully at the old cat, and speaking in as cross a voice as she could manage--and then she scrambled back into the arm-chair, taking the kitten and the worsted with her, and began winding up the ball again. But she didn't get on very fast, as she was talking all the time, sometimes to the kitten, and sometimes to herself. Kitty sat very demurely on her knee, pretending to

 © Excellent English 2012. www.ignitetuition.co.uk

watch the progress of the winding, and now and then putting out one paw and gently touching the ball, as if it would be glad to help, if it might.

"Do you know what tomorrow is, Kitty?" Alice began. "You'd have guessed if you'd been up in the window with me--only Dinah was making you tidy, so you couldn't. I was watching the boys getting in sticks for the bonfire--and it wants plenty of sticks, Kitty! Only it got so cold, and it snowed so, they had to leave off. Never mind, Kitty, we'll go and see the bonfire tomorrow." Here Alice wound two or three turns of the worsted round the kitten's neck, just to see how it would look: this led to a scramble, in which the ball rolled down upon the floor, and yards and yards of it got unwound again.

"Do you know, I was so angry, Kitty," Alice went on as soon as they were comfortably settled again, "when I saw all the mischief you had been doing, I was very nearly opening the window, and putting you out into the snow! And you'd have deserved it, you little mischievous darling! What have you got to say for yourself? Now don't interrupt me!' she went on, holding up one finger. "I'm going to tell you all your faults. Number one: you squeaked twice while Dinah was washing your face this morning. Now you can't deny it, Kitty: I heard you! What's that you say?" (pretending that the kitten was speaking.) "Her paw went into your eye? Well, that's YOUR fault, for keeping your eyes open--if you'd shut them tight up, it wouldn't have happened. Now don't make any more excuses, but listen! Number two: you pulled Snowdrop away by the tail just as I had put down the saucer of milk before her! What, you were thirsty, were you? How do you know she wasn't thirsty too? Now for number three: you unwound every bit of the worsted while I wasn't looking!

That's three faults, Kitty, and you've not been punished for any of them yet. You know I'm saving up all your punishments for Wednesday week-- Suppose they had saved up all MY punishments!" she went on, talking more to herself than the kitten.

Answer the following questions

1) In your own words, explain what the word 'reproachfully' means.

(1 mark)

_____

_____

2) Give one reason why the white kitten could not have been responsible for messing up the worsted ball   **(2 marks)**

_____

_____

_____

_____

3) What do you think the word 'demurely' means?   **(1 mark)**

_____

4) Alice mentions that 'tomorrow' is a special day. What day might it be? Provide **one** reason for your answer using evidence from the text.   **(4 marks)**

_____

_____

_____

5)   What does Alice want to do to punish Kitty?   **(1 mark)**

a. Leave the kitten at home

b. Stop feeding the kitten

c. Leave the kitten outside in the snow

d. Save her punishments for later in the week.

e. Make the kitten wind up the worsted

6) Why is Alice angry at the kitten?   **(1 mark)**

   a. The kitten squealed twice whilst Dinah was washing its face

   b. The kitten unwound the worsted

   c. The kitten pulled Snowdrop away as Alice was about to feed it

   d. The kitten had its eyes open which meant that another cat poked its eye

   e. All of the above.

Writing Task

Imagine Kitty could speak. What would she say? Write a composition that describes the story from her point of view. Your composition should be descriptive, detailed and show your creative thinking skills!

(10 marks)

Have you ever looked after a naughty pet? Write a diary entry describing a day when a pet went crazy!   **(10 marks)**

Write an article for your school magazine about looking after animals. It might be useful to tell readers about your favourite animal and explain why you like this particular animal.   **(10 marks)**

I scored: _____

Comprehension Answers

Alice in Wonderland Answers

1. **B.** Alice was bored of having nothing to do whilst sitting with her sister by the bank.

2. **A.** Protagonist means a leading or major character in a drama, film, play, novel or story.

2. **B.** Alice

3. A description of how Alice feels should include adjectives such as confused, curious, anxious, fearful or apprehensive.

4. '**Burning with curiosity**' implies that upon seeing how peculiar the rabbit was, Alice was immediately determined to find out more about this rather unusual rabbit.

5. **C.** Dialogue and images.

Adventures in Kensington Gardens Answers

1) His father (or father figure)

2) Answer: C. He fears she might die soon

3) Answer B. Cantankerous

4) Subdues means to reduce, quieten or vanquish. Buoyancy means to remain afloat in liquid or to rise in air or gas.

5) Because punching makes David laugh and the narrator loves to hear his son laugh

6) Because she's had an influence on David. Since the day he was born, she has caused him to change his personality and behaviour

 © Excellent English 2012. www.ignitetuition.co.uk

Cyclone Cellar Answers

1) A prairie is a large open area of grassland.

2) Dorothy lives on a farm in Kansas

3) This phrase describes the power of the sun; it's rays are so hot that they turn the previously green grass grey. The sun stops the land from being moist which in turn causes 'little cracks' to run through the land. Full marks should be given to students who provide a solid and concise explanation.

4) Examples of alliterative phrases may include the following: "Big bed," "cyclone cellar," "ladder led," "broke the broad," "so startled," "wail of the wind" and "stern and solemn."

5) The sun has transformed Aunt Em from a young, pretty woman to an aged one who has lost her sparkle. The sun has also caused Uncle Em to age and be less joyous than he once was. Furthermore, the sun has wreaked havoc on the farm land by causing the land to become dry.

Around The World in 80 Days Answers

1) He lived in the 19th century.

2) Phileas' occupation was unknown. We know this because he didn't belong to any legal or occupational groups or clubs which most professionals would have been members of. The only group he belongs to is the Reform Club which isn't an occupational club or group but a social one.

3) The word enigmatical/ enigmatic means difficult to understand or decipher. It's also commonly used to refer to someone or something that is mysterious. It is used to describe Phileas because he is a very mysterious character who reveals very little about himself and surrounds himself with an air of mystery.

 © Excellent English 2012. www.ignitetuition.co.uk

4) Phileas is compared to Byron because they resemble each other/ look alike. However, one thing that makes Phileas different to Byron is that he is more tranquil, peaceful and relaxed than Byron is.

5) Synonyms may include any of the following words or any other words with similar meanings: greedy, rapacious, stingy, grasping, miserly, close-fisted, mean. One mark should be awarded for each correct synonym.

6) Antonyms may include any of the following or suitable alternative words: harmless, innocuous, innocent, guiltless, devoid, sinless. One mark should be given for each correct antonym.

7) Reserved.

8) Yes, he was 'undoubtedly' wealthy. In the text it says that he was generous, not greedy but didn't spend his money unwisely. He gave to others and was cautious with his money. The fact that he was well-travelled also suggests that he was a wealthy man.

9) Any 3 of the following reasons should be awarded 1 mark each: the game suited his quiet nature; the money made from playing the game was used to fund his favourite charities; he enjoyed the challenge; he played for the sake of it.

 © Excellent English 2012. www.ignitetuition.co.uk

Through The Looking Glass Answers

1) To reproach means to blame, criticise or disprove of someone or something.

2) She couldn't have been responsible because she had been washing her face for the past 15 minutes.

3) Demurely means to do something in a reserved, elegant or shy manner. A mark should be given to a definition that is similar to this.

4) From Alice's comments we can deduce that tomorrow is Bonfire's/ Guy Fawkes Night.

5) Answer: D. Save her punishments for later in the week.

6) All of the above.

Writing Task Guidance

An excellent answer worthy of full marks will be descriptive and show a high level of imaginative skills. Students aiming for top marks should write in a style that fits in well with the extract. Accurate punctuation, grammar and spelling should be awarded with additional marks. A high-performing student's work should read as though it's part of (or related to) the extract and should be written to an exceptionally high standard.

7413139R00021

Printed in Great Britain
by Amazon.co.uk, Ltd.,
Marston Gate.